Frank's Guide To Caring For Bonsai

For The Part-Time Enthusiast

Or The Not-So-Competent Hobbyist

By

Frank Weaver

Acknowledgements

To my family, who, for many different reasons, have encouraged me in my quest to improve my Bonsai knowledge and techniques.

I will be forever grateful to my long-term clubs, **Chichester and District Bonsai Society** and **Solent Bonsai**, for the friendship and knowledge that I have received over many years, with a special note for my close friend, now deceased, **Don Ellis (R.I.P.)**.

From the time I first met Don, he came across as having a vast knowledge of bonsai and the extra ability of being able to remember not only the English names of trees but also the Japanese. Always happy to pass on his knowledge, if you had the courage to ask for help.

To **Manor Nursery Garden Centre, Chichester**, with whom a close relationship has enabled our club to grow in numbers for many years, at the same time providing us with the opportunity to put on a superb Annual Bonsai Exhibition, free to the public, for the past 15 years plus. They also allow space for three workshops a year, free to the public, for help and advice.

To **Collette Williams of Collette's Bonsai**. A bonsai friend who has always been of help to me and our club. A very knowledgeable lady who has always found time to pass on her bonsai knowledge when asked for or needed.

Last but by no means least, **my nephew James Elliott**, whose IT and AI skills have transformed years of my notes into this book.

In addition, our clubs have been fortunate over the years to host many talks and demonstrations by a number of very talented bonsai enthusiasts—or, dare I say, **experts**.

This book is designed for the bonsai enthusiast, not for the perfectionist. It is intended to gently guide you throughout the seasons.

The majority of us will never enter a bonsai competition or achieve perfection in our bonsai quest; we simply want to own beautiful trees and enjoy caring for them.

> *"To me, bonsai is part art, part gardening, but mostly a thoroughly therapeutic pastime or hobby. When time or weather permits, it's out in the sun with a cup of tea or a glass of wine, which in itself is a pleasure to behold."*

Not Just for Display

I've purposely designed this book so that it can be used as a diary year after year. There are no pretty pictures, just information on how to make your hobby interesting and your trees last for years to come.

In fact, this book is designed to be used—muddy fingerprints welcome. Mark it, dog-ear it, scribble what worked (or didn't) for you. Your trees will evolve, and your approach should too.

Whether you're just starting out or already pruning like a pro, this book is designed to be your seasonal companion through a bonsai year. It's not about perfection—it's about progress, patience, and enjoying the view.

Contents

Monthly Growth

In the final pages of this book, there is a monthly calendar dedicated to the work needed in caring for our trees during a single month. Think of it like a gardening almanac but smaller, leafier, and slightly more obsessed with roots.

Each monthly section includes practical guidance on:

- **Watering** – what your trees need and when (don't under-water or over-water; damp is better)

- **Feeding** – seasonal nutrition (don't overdo it; liquid feed and slow-release are both good)

- **Repotting** – when to disturb the roots (and when not to)

- **Pruning and trimming** – the fine art of snipping without regret (always leave at least two sets of leaves when pruning, as stripping all leaves from a branch may cause it to die)

- **Wiring** – tree yoga, but with copper (wire as loosely as you can, while still enabling you to get the shape you require)

- **Pests and protection** – keeping your trees healthy and safe (check regularly for pests and fungi)

- **Tools and display** – maintenance and showing off (tastefully; very few tools are needed in the early days, but like all hobbyists, the better you get, the more tools you think you need)

- **Assessment** – tracking progress and noticing change

My Top Tips

Scattered throughout the book, you'll find my top tips. These are little nuggets of practical, honest, and sometimes chuckle-worthy wisdom gathered from over two decades of hands-on bonsai experience, such as:

> *"If you're unsure what to do with a tree, put it in a place where you can see it every day. Sooner or later, the tree will tell you what to do."*

What You'll Need: Not Very Much

A few trees.

A place with some light.

Curiosity.

And either a bonsai toolkit—or my trusty five: florist scissors, an old fork, a chopstick, tweezers, and confidence.

Let's Get Started!

My Journey into Bonsai

I began my journey into bonsai about 25 years ago, when I bought my wife a bonsai tree for her birthday. It was a Chinese elm, and I'm happy to say it's still with us—now about 35 years old. That first tree was the start of something.

When I retired, my family bought me a bonsai lesson. That spark of curiosity soon became a full-blown hobby, and joining a local bonsai club was the best thing I could have done. I also recommend joining the **UK Bonsai Association**—it's free and full of friendly, knowledgeable people.

Through bonsai, I've gained far more than just miniature trees. I've found friendship, peace, and a better way to spend time in the garden. For me, bonsai became an enjoyable, small-scale form of gardening. It gave structure to my seasons, patience to my hands, and clarity to my mind. There's something deeply satisfying about tending a tree that's been with you for years—sometimes even decades.

People often buy a bonsai tree and give up too soon. It dies because nobody told them if it was indoor or outdoor, or how to look after it. The secret is this: bonsai aren't ornaments, they're living things. And we're just the custodians. They will live in a pot for the same length of time that they live in the wild, providing suitable care is given to them.

You don't need expensive tools or years of training to start bonsai. A pair of florist scissors, a bent kitchen fork, and a little courage go a long way. Yes, you'll be nervous at first. But the more you prune, the more it grows. You'll see.

In this book are the notes I've kept and lessons I've learned. I'm not a bonsai master—just an enthusiastic amateur who wants to share what's worked and what hasn't. I hope these tips help you find the same joy I have. And remember: you're growing more than a tree—you're growing patience, beauty, and maybe even yourself.

A Start to Bonsai for the Raw Beginners

Start here if you've never pruned a twig in your life.

What Is Bonsai?

Bonsai literally means *bon* (tree) *sai* (pot): a tree in a pot. But spiritually? It's the art—and craft—of growing trees in small containers while mimicking their natural, majestic form. Think of it as tree-shaping meets meditation... with occasional spider mites.

You're not torturing a tree. You're training it, gently, over time. The goal isn't speed—it's serenity.

Indoor vs Outdoor

Before anything else: figure out where your tree belongs.

This is a reason beginner bonsai die. Thinking about it, how many trees throughout the world grow indoors? Very few, if any. Therefore, if your tree originates from a tropical climate, it will survive indoors; otherwise, like most trees, it grows outdoors.

- **Outdoor bonsai:** Most temperate species (maple, pine, juniper) need seasonal variation—cold winters included. Leave them outside year-round (with protection from extreme cold or frost). Living in the south of the country, I've found that outside in winter, the trees are OK to around zero temperature.

- **Indoor bonsai:** Usually tropical or subtropical species (ficus, Chinese elm, serissa) that need warmth and steady conditions. Keep near good light, not on a windowsill or on top of a radiator.

> *"A lot of trees are lost on windowsills. Don't roast them like a potato."*

Choosing Your First Tree

Start with something:

- Hardy and forgiving (Chinese elm, ficus, cotoneaster)

- Already in good soil (not peat-heavy mush)

- Sold by someone who can tell you if it's indoor or outdoor

Avoid:

- Trees with yellow foliage (often signs of poor health)

- Anything that looks "gift shop perfect"—they're usually neglected stock

Don't Overthink Tools

You don't need a samurai-grade toolkit.

Essential tools:

- Pruning scissors (florist scissors work fine)

- Wire cutters or strong pliers

- A rake or old fork (for root work)

- Tweezers

- A small watering can with a fine rose

Optional extras: chopsticks, soil sieve, spray bottle

Luxury add-ons: concave cutters, jin pliers, repotting sickle, root hook

The Secret to Bonsai?

Water it.

Look at it.

Learn from it.

Repeat.

Your bonsai won't grow overnight—but you might.

My Collected Tips and Wisdom

A lovingly compiled set of practical, philosophical, and occasionally cheeky bonsai truths.

I have spent over two decades growing, pruning, failing, fixing, laughing, and learning. These are his notes—restructured and grouped for easy reference—covering everything from styling and feeding to patience and perspective.

Each block includes my callouts for extra clarity.

Let's start with general tips:

- Avoid the temptation to collect too many trees, or you will not have enough time to give them all sufficient attention.

- Beginners should avoid choosing species with yellow or golden foliage, as this can give a false impression of the tree's health.

- When styling a tree, regularly refer to the front of the tree to avoid making ill-judged pruning decisions.

- Remember that flowers and fruit remain the same size as on a normally grown tree and cannot be reduced.

- If junipers lack good colour, water with an Epsom salts solution; it restores a rich dark green colour.

- If a branch is damaged but not broken off, secure it with sealant; it should repair itself. An animal bandage also works well.

- Leave the removal of major branches until the end of summer when sap flow has reduced; this results in a smaller callus and less sap loss.

- Consider air-layering trees with a poor root system or trunk line; you normally get a much better result after this process.

- When air-layering, add some Marmite to the root growth (vitamin B12).

Pruning and Styling

- Don't be afraid to prune hard. The more you prune, the more it grows.

- Always prune strong terminal buds on ash, sycamore, and horse chestnut—this promotes back budding and finer ramification. Do it on a three-year cycle.

- Trident and other maples tolerate heavy root pruning. Let them grow wild, then cut back to thicken trunks without major scarring.

- Use a white towel or paper to mask a branch before cutting it. This helps you visualise the result before committing.

- Style your tree for you, not for judges. Choose the front that makes you smile in the morning.

> *"The more you prune, the more the tree grows. Once you realise it doesn't die, you get braver."*

Remember to leave at least **two** sets of leaves when pruning to protect the branch.

Feeding and Growth

- Only fertilise during the growing season.

Don't feed:

- Newly repotted trees (wait for new growth)

- Sick plants

- Dormant trees

- Flowering trees while in flower

- Cut back nitrogen- and phosphorus-heavy feeds during autumn.

- Weak liquid feed added to a rainwater tub equals a lazy gardener's dream.

> *"Feeling lazy? Add liquid feed to your rain barrel. Water and feed in one go."*

Repotting and Roots

- Young or small trees: repot yearly

- Medium trees: every two to three years

- Large trees: every three to five years or more

Additional guidance:

- Clean pots thoroughly before repotting.

- Never reduce a heavy root ball all at once; do it over multiple repotting seasons.

- After repotting, don't feed for four weeks. Let the roots settle.

- Wire in drainage gauze to keep pests out and gravel in.

> *"If you're impatient with roots, you'll end up with compost—not a tree."*

Tools and Techniques

- Use florist scissors, kitchen forks, and pliers. Expensive tools are nice, but not necessary.

- Always keep tools clean and sharp. Camellia oil works wonders.

- Clean pots with white vinegar and bicarbonate of soda for stubborn scale.

- Reuse training wire by straightening and storing it properly.

- Always check that existing wire isn't biting into bark— reset or remove as needed.

> *"Most tools aren't essential—unless it's your kettle."*

Pests and Prevention

- Brush off moss and weeds using a toothbrush and diluted vinegar.

- Scale insects: dab them with methylated spirits on a cotton bud.

- Spray junipers with lime sulphur (30:1 mix); cover roots before spraying.

- Always remove dead leaves before winter to avoid mould or fungal build-up.

Climate and Care Philosophy

- Adjust advice to your UK climate—it's very different from Japan or China. Even north and south UK conditions vary greatly.

- Willow trees love moisture—keep in a water tray from spring to autumn.

- Don't collect too many trees too early. Quality over quantity.

- If unsure how to proceed with a tree, put it somewhere visible—inspiration follows observation.

> *"Your best tool is your eyeballs. Put the tree where you'll stare at it often."*

Choosing the Front

My personal view is that choice matters. In bonsai competitions, the "front" of a tree is judged by balance, branch symmetry, trunk angle, nebari (root spread), and visual flow.

But unless you're entering a show, the only front that matters is yours.

> *"Unless you're showing the tree, choose a front that you like. You're the one who wakes up and sees it every morning."*

How to Choose Your Front

1. **Spin it:** Slowly rotate the pot. Look for a trunk angle that feels dynamic—not too straight, not too flat.

2. **Check the roots:** The base of the trunk should feel grounded. Visible surface roots that flare slightly help anchor the tree.

3. **Branch distribution:** Aim for visual depth, not a flat wall of branches.

4. **Trunk character:** Twists, bark texture, or dramatic scars can become highlights. Don't hide them—celebrate them.

5. **Background and light:** If displaying the tree, consider the setting. Light and shadow can change everything.

My Personal View

> *"Don't let someone else tell you which angle is right—unless they water it too."*
>
> *"Even ugly trees have a best side. Sometimes that's the back. But it's still yours."*

Choosing a front is part of the fun. If you change your mind in a year or two, that's fine. Bonsai is always in motion—even if the trees barely move.

Caring for Bonsai in British Climates

Most bonsai books are written with Japan, China, or California in mind. That's lovely—but it's not Yorkshire in February. British weather is wet, mild, unpredictable, and often soggy. Adapting your bonsai care for the UK is essential.

"We've got three seasons: rain, wind, and waiting for the next shower. Bonsai's got to live through all of them."

What Makes the UK Tricky

- High humidity encourages moss, fungus, and root rot

- Frequent rain can over-water trees if drainage isn't ideal

- Wind exposure dries shallow pots faster than expected

- Mild winters can still bring sudden freezes

- Lack of sunlight slows growth for light-loving species

How to Adapt Like a Pro

Drainage is King

- Use open soil mixes (akadama, pumice, pine bark)

- Raise pots off the ground for airflow

- Avoid water-retaining trays in winter

Winter Protection

- Use a cold frame, greenhouse, shed window, or fleece

- Small pots are high-risk in frost

- Remove all dead leaves before storing

Watch the Wind

- Windburn is real—especially on thin-leaved species

- Shelter trees on benches against fences or house walls

Light and Location

- Track where the sun falls in your garden across the year

- Rotate trees every few weeks if one side is fading

Adjust the Advice

If a book says "repot in March" but it's still snowing where you are—wait.

> *"The best bonsai advice is local advice. Don't repot just because Tokyo does."*

Budget Bonsai

How to grow a beautiful bonsai collection without growing your credit card bill.

One of the biggest myths in bonsai is that it's an expensive hobby. Sure, you can spend hundreds on imported trees, carbon-steel tools, and hand-glazed pots. But you don't need to. I started with a birthday tree, a lesson, and kitchen scissors.

> *"Most of what I use came from a drawer, a shed, or someone else's skip."*

My Budget-Friendly Tool Kit

Purpose	Fancy Tool	My Alternative
Pruning	Bonsai scissors	Florist scissors or kitchen shears
Root comb	Root hook	Old fork (bent works best)
Wire cutters	Bonsai wire cutters	Heavy-duty pliers
Soil sifter	Mesh sieve	Garden riddle or colander
Chopstick tool	Bamboo stick or tweezers	Actual chopsticks
Moss brush	Wire brush	Used toothbrush
Drainage mesh	Bonsai grid	Plastic mesh from fruit punnets

Soil on a Budget

My preferred mix:

- 60% akadama
- 40% pumice

I add a small amount of fine pine bark, depending on the type of tree. You can buy in bulk to save money, or, for training trees or why not sift and recycle quality soil:

Cat litter (Alternative budget options) include:

- Non-clumping baked clay type like Tesco Low Dust
- Horticultural grit or crushed lava rock
- Composted bark

Avoid peat-based composts; they retain too much water and compact fast.

Where to Find Trees Cheaply

- Garden centres (look for end-of-season sales)
- Discount supermarkets (they often stock bonsai... badly)
- Online bonsai forums or Facebook groups

- Dig one up! (Legally, of course—your garden or with permission)

- Grow from seed or cuttings (slow but rewarding)

"Some of my best trees came from the clearance shelf. Bit of love, bit of pruning, and they show you what they were hiding."

Final Advice: Spend Less, Learn More

The most valuable thing in bonsai isn't your pot or your scissors—it's your patience. Money can't buy experience.

Start small. Start scrappy. Start now.

My Favourite Trees

Why Junipers and Cotoneasters win year after year.

Over the decades, I have worked with many species—some forgiving, some finicky, some just plain moody. But two trees have always stood out as firm favourites: **Junipers** and **Cotoneasters**.

They're hardy, expressive, beautiful year-round, and offer lots of options for styling. They also forgive a few beginner mistakes—which is good, because we all make them.

Junipers: Sculptors' Delight

Why I love them:

- Evergreen with strong character

- Respond well to wiring and shaping

- Produce beautiful deadwood (jin and shari)

- Can be styled into dramatic, sweeping shapes

Care notes:

- Need full sun

- Don't overwater—they hate wet feet

- Enjoy gentle pruning, not constant nibbling

- Like being left alone a bit between styling sessions

"Junipers don't need babysitting—they need you to stop fussing and let them look majestic."

Cotoneasters: The All-Year Friend

Why I love them:

- Tiny leaves perfect for small-scale trees

- White flowers in spring, red berries in autumn

- Tough, resilient, and respond well to pruning

- Easy to root from cuttings

Care notes:

- Deciduous or semi-evergreen (varies by species and climate)

- Likes full sun or partial shade

- Keep moist but well-drained

Can thicken quickly when grown freely for a year or two.

"Cotoneasters give you flowers, fruit, and fun. What more do you want from a twig in a pot?"

Final Thought

Bonsai is about relationship—not perfection. My favourites might not be yours, but these two species have proven their worth over and over, across seasons and styles.

Try one. Or both. You might just find yourself planting a few more before the year is out.

The Art of Not Rushing

What bonsai teaches us when we're too busy to notice we're learning.

Bonsai takes time. Not Instagram-time. Real time.

A year to settle. Two to shape. Five to mature. A decade to really start looking like something special.

That might sound slow. But it's not dead time—it's *growing time.*

> *"We're so busy rushing about, we forget to sit and watch something grow. Bonsai fixes that."*

What You Learn While You Wait

Patience

You prune a branch—then wait a season to see if it worked. You wire a trunk—then wait years for the curve to settle. Bonsai stretches your timeline until the rush fades.

Acceptance

Not every tree grows the way you want. Some die. Some surprise you. Some come back after you thought they were goners. Bonsai teaches you to roll with it—and to listen more than you push.

Perspective

You start seeing time in seasons, not days. You begin noticing buds in February and new growth in April. You spot insects most people miss. You're no longer just looking at trees—you're seeing *through* them.

Trees in Training. And People Too.

Bonsai trees are never finished—they're always in training. So are we. You don't "master" bonsai. You just keep showing up, trimming a little, watering a little, and learning a bit more every time.

"Bonsai helps you age gracefully. Not bad for a stick in a pot."

Appendix

Soil, Repotting & Feeding options

A quick-reference guide to keep your trees happy underground.

Soil Mix Basics

Bonsai soil must do three things:

1. Drain well
2. Retain moisture
3. Provide aeration

There is no one-size-fits-all soil, but here's a solid all-rounder:

My Favourite Mix

- 60% Akadama (holds moisture, breaks down slowly)
- 40% Pumice (drainage + root oxygen)

Small handful of fine pine bark (lightens the mix, adds organic matter)

> *"It's like baking—everyone's got a mix they swear by. But mine's light, drains well, and doesn't give you a hernia carrying the pot."*

Repotting Schedule

Tree Age	*Repotting Frequency*
1–3 years (young trees)	Every year
4–7 years (developing trees)	Every two years
8+ years (mature trees)	Every three to five years, or as needed

Tips

- Always clean pots thoroughly before use

- Never root-prune too aggressively all at once

- Use drainage mesh to keep soil in and pests out

- Let repotted trees rest — **no feeding for 4 weeks**

Feeding Dos and Don'ts

Do:

- Feed during the growing season

- Use low-nitrogen fertiliser in spring and autumn

- Use organic liquid feeds little and often

- Resume feeding only once new growth appears after repotting

Don't:

- Feed trees in flower

- Feed sick trees

- Feed dormant trees

- Feed immediately after repotting

> *"Feeding is like tea—too strong, too often, and you'll upset the roots."*

Glossary

Glossary: Bonsai Terms Made Simple

- **Akadama** – A clay-like granular soil from Japan, great for water retention and root health.

- **Back budding** – New buds that grow further back on a branch, often encouraged by pruning.

- **Callus** – The healing tissue that forms over a wound or cut.

- **Cascading** – A style where the trunk drops below the edge of the pot.

- **Deadwood (Jin/Shari)** – Artistic use of natural-looking dead branches or trunk areas to suggest age.

- **Defoliation** – Removing leaves to encourage smaller growth or multiple flushes in a season.

- **Nebari** – Surface root flare at the base of the trunk. Often a sign of age and stability.

- **Ramification** – Fine branching—the more, the better for mature, detailed trees.

- **Repotting** – Changing the soil and pruning roots, done every few years depending on age and health.

- **Shohin** – A category of small bonsai, typically under 20cm tall.

- **Wiring** – Applying wire to shape or hold branches in position while they grow.

"Don't get too tangled in jargon. A healthy tree doesn't care what it's called—just how you treat it."

Monthly Calendar

Bonsai in January

Winter is here and most deciduous trees will have dropped their leaves. Their true structure is now revealed—branches, ramification, trunk line—all visible for evaluation. This is a time for quiet assessment. The tree's silhouette is clean, and the distractions of foliage are gone.

Evergreens will begin to dull. The rich green of pines or junipers might lose some lustre, a natural response to reduced sunlight and colder temperatures. Don't panic—this seasonal shift is part of their rest cycle.

Trees requiring winter protection should already be under cover, in cold frames, greenhouses, or sheltered spots. In the UK, trees such as Chinese elm, trident maple, and ficus need protection from frost. Junipers, pines, and many native species are hardier, but even they benefit from wind shielding and moisture control.

Watering slows, but it doesn't stop. Even in dormancy, trees lose moisture through their branches and need water—just far less of it. Rainfall, dew, and melting frost might cover the basics outdoors. For covered trees, check soil every few days. If it's bone dry, water gently. Never allow bonsai to become waterlogged; stagnant moisture plus cold equals root rot.

Now is the time to check wiring applied in late summer or autumn. The branches may have thickened. If the wire is beginning to bite, remove it carefully. Don't leave wire on until spring—cut it off in segments rather than unwinding if the bark is tight.

Clean your tools. Disinfect shears, oil your cutters, and organise your supplies. Bonsai practice is as much about preparation as action. January is the deep breath before repotting season begins.

If you're lucky enough to have a large indoor workspace or cold frame with light, you can begin shaping work on hardy species. But avoid major pruning unless you're experienced. Let the trees sleep. Plan your spring.

"Stand back from each tree in winter. Turn it. Look from below. What shape does it really have? This is the tree's skeleton—its truth."

January checklist:

- Minimal watering, only as needed

- Check wire for bite; remove if necessary

- Plan for repotting (prepare soil, mesh, pots)

- Organise and clean tools

- Observe branch structure for future styling

This is the bonsai winter: still, cold, preparatory. There is beauty in the bones.

My Personal Notes

Bonsai in February

February is the bridge between deep dormancy and the first signs of spring. For many species, buds are still tight, but roots are beginning to stir below the soil line. This is the month when repotting begins in earnest—timing is everything.

Repotting is not just about giving your tree new soil. It is a critical health procedure. Roots are trimmed to encourage fine root growth, old compacted soil is replaced with a fresh, well-draining mix, and the tree is reset into position for the next stage of its development.

The best time to repot most deciduous trees is when buds are just beginning to swell—before they open. If you wait too long, the tree will be in active growth and the shock of repotting can do damage. For evergreens, wait a little longer. Many conifers prefer late winter to early spring for root work.

Start with your healthiest, most vigorous trees. Weak trees should not be repotted unless absolutely necessary. When removing the tree from its pot, take time to examine the roots. Trim circling or thick roots, untangle and spread the finer ones. Always use clean tools and fresh soil.

After repotting, water thoroughly. Then protect the tree from frost and wind for at least two weeks. A greenhouse or cold frame is ideal. Avoid feeding until new growth appears.

If you're not repotting, February is still useful. Clean pots, prepare soil mixes, label trees by repotting priority. Check wire again—late winter growth can still cause biting.

You can also begin shaping or structural pruning on some species. Deciduous trees respond well to early shaping before sap rises too strongly. But don't overdo it. If in doubt, wait until March.

This is also a good time to evaluate your collection. Do you have too many trees to properly care for? Is one tree failing in its pot because it's never been styled or trained? Use this quieter time to make decisions. Letting go of a tree can be as valuable as acquiring one.

"Repot with calm hands and a sharp eye. The roots will tell you everything about the tree's future."

February checklist:

- Begin repotting (when buds begin to swell)

- Trim roots and refresh soil

- Avoid frost after repotting

- Prepare wire and tools

- Plan collection layout for the growing season

In February, you move from reflection into action. The tree is preparing to grow—so should you.

Do not feed for four weeks after repotting.

My Personal Notes

Bonsai in March

March is the awakening. Buds swell, leaves unfurl, and the entire bonsai bench begins to stir with life. The light returns, the air warms, and the season of growth begins. It is a time of energy—but it must be managed carefully.

Repotting continues for many species in early March. If you haven't yet repotted your deciduous trees and their buds are still unopened or just beginning to swell, now is your last chance. For conifers and evergreens, this may be the preferred time—especially if you're in a colder climate where February was still deep winter.

Trees that were repotted in February should now be protected from wind and frost, but allowed full light. As soon as new shoots appear, resume a light watering schedule and prepare to begin feeding—though only with mild fertiliser at half strength until the tree is fully active.

Now is the time to monitor wire carefully. With the surge of growth, branches can thicken rapidly, and wire can cut in deeply if not checked. If there is any sign of biting, remove the wire. It's better to rewire later than to leave scars.

Pruning begins in March, particularly on deciduous trees. Structural pruning—removing unwanted thick branches or correcting the basic silhouette—should be done before the tree is fully in leaf. Once in leaf, move to maintenance pruning only.

Don't overwork your trees in spring. New growth is fragile, and too much interference can exhaust the tree. Style lightly. Let the tree lead.

You can begin wiring new growth if it is strong enough to hold a shape. Be gentle. Young shoots are tender and bruise easily.

For flowering bonsai—such as quince, flowering cherry, or forsythia—allow them to bloom before shaping. Enjoy the flowers. Then prune back to maintain form and encourage next year's blossoms.

Begin feeding trees that are showing strong growth. Use a balanced, organic fertiliser at half strength every two weeks. Increase strength in April as the tree's appetite grows.

"When a tree wakes up, it doesn't want shouting. It wants encouragement."

March checklist:

- Finish repotting (especially evergreens)

- Begin gentle feeding

- Start structural pruning on deciduous trees

- Monitor and remove biting wire

- Protect tender growth from late frost

March is energy, but not recklessness. Spring rewards the patient grower—those who watch closely and act with care. Let the tree stretch, and stretch alongside it.

My Personal Notes

Bonsai in April

April is when the bonsai bench comes alive. Leaves unfurl in full, candles extend on pines, and the first real wave of spring growth arrives. This is a month of momentum—but that momentum must be directed wisely. Trees are eager, but if left alone, they may grow out of balance or develop faults that take years to correct.

Watering becomes a daily practice again. The rising temperature and increasing foliage mean higher transpiration. Observe each tree. Trees in smaller pots dry out faster. Trees recently repotted may not need as much water until roots re-establish. Check every day, but only water when the soil needs it. Avoid the trap of routine—water based on need, not habit.

Feeding begins in earnest. Most bonsai can now be fed every two weeks with a balanced fertiliser. Use an organic option if you can. For flowering or fruiting species, use a fertiliser with lower nitrogen until flowers fade, then return to balance. For conifers, avoid strong feeding until late spring.

Pinching and pruning are essential now. New shoots extend rapidly and must be pinched back to maintain shape and encourage ramification. On deciduous trees, pinch back after two to four leaves have emerged, depending on the species and your goals. Don't remove all the new growth at once—leave some energy for the tree to continue photosynthesis.

Conifers should not be pinched yet—wait until May or June when candles begin to harden. For now, focus on monitoring and planning.

Watch for pests. Aphids, spider mites, and scale insects emerge now. Use neem oil or insecticidal soap at the first sign of trouble. Examine the undersides of leaves and look for distorted growth or fine webbing.

Wiring can resume cautiously. Trees that were recently repotted or pruned may not respond well to wiring, so choose healthy, stable trees. Young growth wires easily, but is also easily damaged. Use gentle curves, wide spacing, and light aluminium wire.

You may begin rotating trees for even light exposure. Trees that face a window or grow under artificial lights can become lopsided quickly in spring.

> *"Growth is the tree's language. Watch how it reaches, then help it reach better."*

April checklist:

- Daily watering checks

- Full feeding schedule begins

- Pinch and prune new growth

- Monitor for pests

- Begin gentle wiring on strong trees

- Rotate trees for even growth

April is about response. The tree is speaking through growth—your role is to understand, support, and guide it. Each cut, pinch, or pause shapes not just the tree's form, but its future.

My Personal Notes

Bonsai in May

May is the month of fullness. Leaves have hardened, shoots extend with confidence, and your trees are in active conversation with the sun, water, and soil. This is the time for refinement. The rush of spring has passed, and now comes the art of control without suppression.

For deciduous trees, continue with maintenance pruning. Cut back extended shoots to maintain silhouette and encourage fine branching. If a tree has grown beyond its design, don't shear it all back in one session—stagger the work across several days to avoid shocking the system.

For maples, be mindful of leaf burn. As sunlight intensifies, delicate species such as Japanese maple may show crispy edges if exposed to midday rays. Provide filtered light or slight shade if needed, especially for red or variegated cultivars.

Conifers begin their shaping season now. Pine candles should be monitored closely. Once the new growth has elongated but before it hardens, you can begin pinching. Use fingers, not scissors, and remove only the central strongest candles while leaving the side shoots. This encourages balanced energy and reduces coarse growth.

You can also begin wiring on conifers now. Their growth has firmed enough to hold shape, and wiring can direct this energy into the tree's long-term structure. Always use care—conifer bark is more delicate than it appears, especially on young branches.

Feeding continues. If growth is strong, increase fertiliser strength slightly. For flowering trees, switch to a higher-phosphorus mix after bloom to support fruit or seed development, or return to a balanced formula for continued vegetative growth.

Watch for pests and fungal issues, especially in dense foliage. Improve air circulation around your trees. Remove excess moss build-up at the base to prevent moisture retention and allow inspection of the surface roots.

You may defoliate some deciduous trees if the leaves have grown large and you wish to encourage smaller, finer foliage. This is advanced work and should only be done on healthy trees. Partial defoliation is safer than full. Don't defoliate weak or recently repotted trees.

> *"Now that the tree is growing, don't get greedy. Let it keep something for itself."*

May checklist:

- Maintenance pruning on deciduous trees

- Begin pine candle pinching

- Wire conifers carefully

- Adjust feeding strength as needed

- Manage sun exposure for sensitive species

- Watch for fungus and insects

May is refinement. The tree knows what it wants to do. Your role is to guide, not to overwhelm. Each decision now builds the shape of summer—and the strength of autumn.

My Personal Notes

Bonsai in June

June is summer's doorway. The days are long, growth is active, and your trees have found their rhythm. This is a month of refinement and health—of watching closely, responding quickly, and staying consistent. The urgent work of spring is behind you, but vigilance is just as important now.

Watering is critical. Hot days and high foliage density mean trees dry out quickly, sometimes within hours. Check moisture levels twice daily during heatwaves. Water deeply in the morning, and again in the late afternoon if needed. Avoid watering at night unless necessary, as cool, damp conditions can invite fungal issues.

Feeding continues at full strength. Apply fertiliser every two weeks or use a slow-release method. For trees in development, feed generously to encourage growth. For refined trees, reduce nitrogen and focus on phosphorus and potassium to promote finer twigs, colour, and strength.

Pine work continues. By now, many black pine candles have hardened. This is the time to decandle—removing the entire spring growth to encourage a second flush of shorter, more compact needles. Decandling should only be done on healthy, vigorous trees, and timing must be precise. It's best performed in mid to late June, depending on your local climate. Red and white pines are not decandled in the same way—handle them with different techniques or avoid entirely unless you're experienced.

Junipers can be pinched or lightly pruned to maintain form. Avoid cutting back into old wood that has no foliage—it won't regenerate. Instead, target tips or gently wire to reposition.

Wiring can still be done, but monitor closely for swelling. Summer growth thickens quickly, and wire marks are harder to heal in warm weather. For deciduous trees, consider removing wire completely and pruning instead.

Fungal issues become more common in June. Watch for black spots, mildew, or unexplained dieback. Improve air circulation by thinning foliage or repositioning trees. Use organic fungicides or neem oil as a preventive measure.

Insects are also more active. Aphids, spider mites, scale, and caterpillars can cause significant damage in summer. Check leaf undersides and branch crotches. A strong jet of water can remove pests, or use insecticidal soap for persistent issues.

You can begin summer defoliation on certain species. On strong, healthy deciduous trees such as maples or hornbeams, removing large leaves encourages smaller second flushes and better ramification. Only defoliate in good weather, and never defoliate a stressed or weak tree.

> *"June is where the tree shows you how strong it really is. Don't interrupt—guide."*

June checklist:

- Water daily, sometimes twice

- Full feeding schedule continues

- Decandle black pines (only if vigorous)

- Pinch junipers; monitor wiring

- Watch for pests and fungus

- Begin controlled defoliation on strong trees

June is about presence. You don't need to interfere constantly, but you do need to show up. Summer strength comes from quiet, repeated care—and knowing when to act and when to wait.

My Personal Notes

Bonsai in July

July is peak summer. Growth slows compared to spring, but the heat brings its own challenges. This is a month of stability, vigilance, and subtle intervention. Your trees are holding the energy they built in spring—now it's about helping them conserve it and preparing them for the slower second half of the year.

Watering is still your most important task. Pots can dry out rapidly in full sun. In very hot weather, water in the early morning and again in the late afternoon. Use shade netting or move trees to slightly shadier spots during heatwaves, especially species prone to leaf burn such as Japanese maples or azaleas.

Humidity trays or gravel beds can help with microclimate control, especially for indoor or greenhouse bonsai. Just be sure they don't trap standing water beneath pots.

Feeding continues, but moderate it based on the tree's behaviour. If growth is slowing, switch to a lower-nitrogen fertiliser or extend the interval between feedings. Refined trees need less. Trees in development can still be fed regularly, but watch for signs of overfeeding—coarse growth, overly long internodes, or dark, oversized leaves.

Maintenance pruning is ongoing. Remove unwanted shoots and pinch back new growth to preserve shape. On flowering or fruiting trees, begin to thin fruit if it's weighing down branches. The goal is to preserve structure and not exhaust the tree.

Wiring should be checked weekly. Summer swelling can bite wire into bark quickly. If wire is beginning to mark, remove it even if the branch hasn't fully set. Scars from summer wire are difficult to heal and can permanently ruin bark texture.

Continue pest and fungus checks. Spider mites thrive in dry heat and can defoliate a bonsai in days. If foliage looks dull, stippled, or dusty, inspect with a magnifying glass. Treat early. Caterpillars and beetles may also be more active—inspect trees after rainfall or windy days.

Defoliation can still be performed on suitable trees, especially in the first half of the month. Avoid defoliation if a heatwave is coming. Defoliated trees need ideal conditions—warmth, light, and consistent moisture—to recover quickly and flush again before autumn.

You can also begin light root pruning on tropical indoor species such as ficus or jade if needed. These species respond well to summer root work and recover quickly, especially if grown indoors or under controlled conditions.

> *"You can't grow a tree on worry. If you've done your part, trust it to do the rest."*

July checklist:

- Maintain a consistent watering schedule

- Adjust feeding to match growth

- Prune to maintain shape and remove excess fruit

- Monitor wire for swelling and remove as needed

- Treat pests and fungus promptly

- Defoliate only strong trees and avoid during extreme heat

July is resilience. Your tree knows how to grow—your job is to protect that effort. The more you observe now, the fewer problems you'll face in autumn. Let the tree mature. Let the growth harden. Let summer settle in.

My Personal Notes

Bonsai in August

August is the heart of late summer—hot, dry, and mature. Growth begins to slow, especially in temperate species. The flush of spring has long passed, and now trees begin to consolidate energy, thicken wood, and set buds for the coming year. For the bonsai practitioner, this is a time for refinement and readiness.

Watering remains essential. While the days may be slightly shorter than in July, the heat often persists or even intensifies. Trees in small pots, shallow pots, or with dense foliage will still dry quickly. Water deeply and thoroughly, ensuring the entire root mass is moistened. Don't just dampen the surface.

Continue to use rainwater where possible, and watch for limescale build-up on pots or soil surfaces if using hard tap water. Flush the soil occasionally with extra water to wash out any accumulated salts.

Feeding should now shift. By mid to late August, most bonsai—especially those in refinement—benefit from a lower-nitrogen feed to prepare for autumn. This reduces soft, leggy growth and supports wood development and bud setting. Continue feeding trees in development more generously, but taper off if they begin to push unwanted late-season growth.

Wiring should be checked closely. Branches thicken rapidly in summer and can bite into bark before you notice. Remove any tight or marking wire. You can rewire in autumn if necessary. If applying new wire, do so gently—hot wood can bruise easily and does not always set well in high heat.

This is a good time for light thinning. Remove excess inner foliage to allow light and air into the canopy. This improves back budding and reduces fungal risk, especially in dense trees such as junipers or hornbeams.

You may still perform minor leaf pruning on deciduous trees to tidy their appearance or encourage light second flushes. Avoid heavy defoliation this late in the season unless working with tropicals.

If you've performed summer defoliation earlier in the season, monitor regrowth. Thin any overly dense clusters and maintain balance in the silhouette.

Tropical and indoor bonsai such as ficus, serissa, and jade may still be in active growth. These can be repotted or root-pruned if needed, especially if kept in warm indoor environments.

This is also a time to prepare for autumn work. Begin reviewing each tree's development and noting which may need wiring, potting adjustments, or heavy pruning in the months ahead.

> *"When the tree slows down, that's your cue to step back. Let the year catch up."*

August checklist:

- Water deeply and consistently

- Shift feeding to lower nitrogen

- Remove tight wire; inspect bark

- Lightly thin dense foliage

- Begin autumn planning

- Repot tropicals if required

August is reflection in action. You're not pushing the tree now—you're observing, maintaining, and allowing it to store energy. In bonsai, as in nature, not every season is for expansion. Some are for strengthening. August is one of them.

My Personal Notes

Bonsai in September

September is transition. The heat begins to fade, the light softens, and your trees respond by slowing their growth. For many species, this is the beginning of their preparation for dormancy. New buds form. Wood hardens. Leaves begin to darken and, for some, blush with the first signs of autumn colour. This is a month for preparation and observation.

Watering should remain consistent but may need slight adjustment. Cooler nights and shorter days slow evaporation. Be attentive—overwatering becomes a greater risk now, especially if rainfall increases. Don't fall into autopilot. Feel the soil, lift the pot, and water only when necessary.

Feeding continues but should now be with low-nitrogen fertiliser for all trees. The focus shifts from growth to strength—potassium and phosphorus help harden wood, develop roots, and set strong buds for spring. Fertilise every two to three weeks or use slow-release pellets to support a steady, gentle intake.

Avoid heavy pruning now. Cuts made in September may not heal before winter, leaving trees vulnerable to disease or dieback. Light shaping or leaf thinning is fine, especially to allow more light into interior branches. If a branch absolutely must be removed, do it early in the month and seal the cut with paste.

Conifers, especially junipers and pines, may be wired now. Their growth has slowed and the wood begins to harden, making it easier to set shape. Wire gently, with wide coils, and avoid trapping moisture beneath the wire, which can invite fungal issues in cooler weather.

Check wiring applied earlier in the season—particularly on deciduous trees. Branches may have thickened quietly and wire could be scarring. Remove any suspect wire before bark damage occurs. Autumn is not the time to take risks with wire marks.

Now is a good time to repot tropicals or indoor species before they come indoors. For temperate species, resist the urge to repot—even if the tree seems sluggish. The root system is moving towards dormancy, and repotting now can set it back.

Start preparing winter quarters. Clean your greenhouse, cold frame, or sheltered area. Repair broken panes, check for pests, test heaters if used, and make sure ventilation is available. Winter protection must be dry, cool, and well aired—not sealed and stagnant.

> *"The tree is closing the year. Don't open new wounds unless you must."*

September checklist:

- Adjust watering for cooler conditions

- Feed with low-nitrogen fertiliser

- Avoid heavy pruning

- Wire conifers if needed

- Remove wire from deciduous trees

- Prepare winter shelters

- Repot tropicals before moving indoors

September is the beginning of the end. But endings in bonsai are not abrupt—they're gradual, patient, and full of meaning. Every bud set now is a promise for spring. Every action you take prepares the tree for its long winter sleep. This is the month where thoughtfulness matters most.

My Personal Notes

Bonsai in October

October is the month of colour and quiet. For many deciduous species, this is when the most stunning displays appear—vibrant reds, oranges, and yellows that briefly turn your bonsai bench into a miniature forest ablaze with autumn. But beneath this beauty, the tree is already turning inward. It is preparing for rest. Your work now shifts to support that transition.

Watering must be reduced but not abandoned. As temperatures fall, trees require less moisture, but they must never be allowed to fully dry out. Rainfall may cover much of your watering needs for outdoor trees, but sheltered or indoor trees will still need monitoring. Cold, wet roots are vulnerable to rot, so drainage must remain excellent.

Feeding should cease for temperate outdoor trees by mid-October. Continued feeding after this point risks encouraging soft late growth that won't harden before frost. If you've been feeding with low-nitrogen fertiliser in September, the tree should have what it needs to store energy over winter.

Wiring can continue on conifers and some deciduous trees that have dropped their leaves, especially if you are styling before winter. With no leaves in the way, the structure is visible and easier to assess. Just be cautious—bark is often more brittle in colder weather. Avoid wiring in freezing temperatures, and ensure that freshly wired trees are protected from extreme conditions.

Fungal issues can still appear, especially as falling leaves accumulate on soil surfaces. Remove leaf litter promptly to avoid mould. Check for pests hiding in crevices as they seek shelter for winter.

Begin moving tender species to their winter quarters. Tropicals must be indoors before night-time temperatures drop below 10°C. Acclimatise them slowly to the indoor environment by reducing light and moisture gradually. Avoid placing them directly near heaters or draughty windows.

Outdoor trees that require partial protection—such as young maples, trident maples, and Chinese elms—can be moved into cold frames or unheated greenhouses later in the month. Do not bring them into warmth unless absolutely necessary. They need the cold period to reset their seasonal cycle.

Tool maintenance becomes a focus now. Clean, sharpen, and oil all tools before winter storage. Empty old soil bags, clean pots, and restock any supplies needed for spring. This is the perfect time to reflect, organise, and prepare.

> *"October is when trees show you who they really are. Not in flowers. Not in fruit. Just in their colours and their bones."*

October checklist:

- Reduce watering; monitor closely

- Stop feeding by mid-month

- Wire bare trees where needed

- Clear fallen leaves to prevent fungus

- Move tropicals indoors

- Prepare winter protection

- Clean and store tools

October is appreciation. Your work slows, but your attention deepens. You walk the bench not with clippers, but with quiet eyes. This is when you learn to see the tree—not as it was, or will be, but exactly as it is now.

My Personal Notes

Bonsai in November

November is the beginning of stillness. Most deciduous trees have dropped their leaves, leaving behind bare branches that reveal their true structure. The bright colours of October give way to silhouettes, shadow, and rest. For the bonsai grower, this is a time of observation, maintenance, and subtle care—not of intervention.

Watering needs drop significantly, but they don't disappear. Even dormant trees require occasional watering to prevent the roots from drying out. Trees under cover won't benefit from rainfall, so check soil moisture weekly and water only when needed. Trees kept outside may need little help, but watch for drying winds that can strip moisture from bare branches.

Feeding stops entirely for all temperate outdoor species. The trees are no longer taking up nutrients, and applying fertiliser now can do more harm than good. Indoor or tropical species still growing under lights may continue on a light feeding schedule, but always observe first—never feed by routine alone.

This is an excellent time for structural analysis. With leaves gone, you can clearly see branch taper, movement, spacing, and flaws. Take notes, sketch outlines, or photograph trees from all sides to plan future work. Resist the urge to cut unless you're very confident—most pruning should wait until late winter or early spring.

Wiring may still be done on conifers or bare deciduous trees, but with care. Cold branches are less flexible and more prone to breakage. If wiring in November, do so on a mild day and avoid pushing tight curves. Wide, gentle movements are safest now.

Cleanliness becomes critical. Remove any fallen leaves, fruit, or debris from soil surfaces. These can harbour pests or encourage fungal infections during the damp season. Clean the pots as well—scrub off algae and mineral deposits to keep the display clean and the roots healthy.

If using a greenhouse or cold frame, monitor temperature and airflow. A sealed environment can easily become too humid, inviting mould or mildew. Ventilate regularly on dry days and avoid direct sunlight that can cause temperature spikes.

Tropicals and indoor species should now be fully inside. Give them the best light you can—south-facing windows or supplemental grow lights work well. Water sparingly and increase humidity through trays or gentle misting. These trees may rest, or they may continue to grow slowly, depending on species and conditions.

> *"Don't be fooled. A sleeping tree is not a dead tree. It's gathering strength you can't yet see."*

November checklist:

- Reduce watering further, but monitor carefully

- Do not feed temperate trees

- Assess structure and make plans

- Wire gently if needed, on warm days

- Clean soil surfaces and pots

- Manage winter shelter ventilation

- Care for tropicals indoors

November is humility. It reminds us that growth isn't always visible. That sometimes the most important changes are happening beneath the surface. The bonsai grower learns to wait here—to watch the stillness and know that it's part of the rhythm. Not every task has a tool. Some tasks just require time.

My Personal Notes

Bonsai in December

December is the quietest month in the bonsai calendar. It is a time of rest for both tree and grower. Your trees are now fully dormant—especially the temperate deciduous species—and there is little to do in terms of training or styling. But there is always something to observe, something to care for, something to prepare.

Watering is minimal. Depending on your climate and whether your trees are kept outdoors or under cover, you may go days or even a week between waterings. But don't let this lull lead to neglect. Check the soil periodically. Use a chopstick or lift the pot to assess moisture. Water only if the soil is dry, and always do so gently to avoid shocking cold roots.

Trees in cold frames, greenhouses, or sheltered areas may dry out faster due to insulation from rain and wind. Ventilate these spaces regularly to prevent condensation, fungal growth, or stale air. If you use heaters for tropicals, monitor temperatures closely—extreme fluctuations can do more harm than steady cold.

Feeding has stopped. Your temperate bonsai do not need nutrients at this time. For tropical or indoor trees still growing under lights, maintain a minimal feeding schedule only if there is active growth.

This is a good time to check wire on deciduous trees. With no leaves to obscure your view, you can clearly see where wire may be biting in. Remove it gently if necessary. Cold weather makes bark more brittle, so always work slowly and with warm, dry hands.

Tool care is a fitting task for winter. Clean, sharpen, and oil your tools. Organise them so you're ready when spring returns. Check your soil supplies, restock mesh, wire, and labels, and prepare for repotting season well in advance—it arrives faster than you think.

You can also reflect on the year's progress. Go through photos of your trees from each season. Look at how they've changed. What worked? What didn't? Which trees need repotting? Which need wiring, restyling, or rest?

For the passionate grower, December is also a month for reading, learning, and planning. Explore bonsai books, watch demonstrations, or revisit your own notes. You may not be cutting or wiring, but you can still grow.

> *"The trees are sleeping. That doesn't mean you have to. This is where the next season begins—in your mind."*

December checklist:

- Water sparingly, only when needed

- Maintain ventilation in shelters

- Monitor for pests or fungal build-up

- Remove wire from dormant trees if biting

- Clean, sharpen, and organise tools

- Reflect and plan for the coming year

December is patience. It reminds you that bonsai is not a project with an end date—it is a lifelong practice. In this stillness, in the quiet spaces between seasons, the bonsai grower learns the true rhythm of the art. Not every month is for action. Some are simply for care. And care, in bonsai, is never wasted.

My Personal Notes

To finalise, we need:

Community and Resources

Join a Club

- **UK Bonsai Association** (free to join) – great for advice, events, and camaraderie

- A full list of Bonsai Clubs are available on **UK Bonsai Association** Site

Local clubs are often listed via the Federation of British Bonsai Societies (FoBBS)

Lastly, enjoy your new talent, your trees, your club, and your many new friends!

www.ingramcontent.com/pod-product-compliance
Lightning Source LLC
Chambersburg PA
CBHW050038040726
47599CB00015B/1739